D1616076

maker.

DIY
Sustainable
Projects

Acknowledgements

To every educator, artist and maker who shares and teaches their process, I'm so lucky to learn from you. Thanks for making this planet a more inspiring place to live.

Published in 2021 by Welbeck
An imprint of Welbeck Non-fiction Limited, part of
Welbeck Publishing Group
20 Mortimer Street
London W1T 3JW

A CIP catalogue record for this book is available from the British Library
ISBN 978 1 78739 397 4

Printed in Dubai
10 9 8 7 6 5 4 3 2 1

maker.

DIY
Sustainable
Projects

15 CRAFT PROJECTS
FOR ECO-FRIENDLY LIVING

Audrey Love

WELBECK

maker.

DIY
Sustainable Projects

Contents

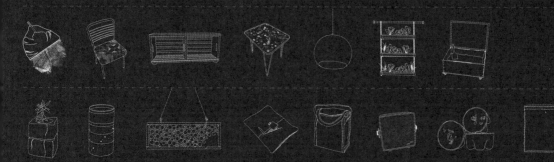

11. Tablet sleeve from a sweater – 108

Forever losing your stylus or forgetting your charger? Keep your tablet and all its accessories in this neat and functional sleeve made from an old sweater.

12. Insulated lunch bag – 116

Using unconventional materials, this project will show you how to turn shipping material into a reusable lunch bag.

13. Upcycled radio – 126

With some basic electronics knowledge, you too can turn this classic speaker into a modern Bluetooth radio.

14. Shampoo and conditioner bars – 136

Using natural botanicals and reused moulds, these shampoo and conditioner bars are a win-win for sustainability and functionality (plus they smell fantastic).

15. Reusable bulk food bags – 146

Made from lightweight nylon, these durable bulk food bags are perfect for all your freshly bought produce.

Introduction

You know, the planet is really quite lucky to have you. Yes, you! Just by picking up this book today, you showed the Earth that you respect the life-giving resources it provides, and that you are willing to do the work to make our world a more sustainable place to live! So, thank you! You're awesome!

No matter where you are on your personal sustainability journey, this book aims to inspire you to reuse everyday objects in creative ways and to create a range of eco-friendly projects for your home and garden. If humans are going to be able to continue living a well-balanced life on Earth, it's time to get serious about the ways we repair and give back to the environment. With previous generations irresponsibly plundering the environment of native plants, ground water and petroleum in the name of rapid development for centuries, humans have splintered the delicate interconnections on which our ecosystems rely. It is this generation's responsibility to undo some of the damage that the last many hundreds of years of industrialization has caused.

This book is a way to create rituals around sustainable practices, contextualizing how individual behaviour and making greener choices within your environment scales to bigger and bigger communities. Making your own soap, growing your own food, etc. – these are small modifications. Societally, we're on the edge of making major adjustments to the way we live, communicate, eat and travel to keep our planet habitable.

You may be asking yourself, "What is considered to be a green material to use?" Sustainability in your home means buying food that has been grown close to your home, or better yet, grown AT your own home. Making greener choices applies to anything that you give a second life to and keep out of a landfill. This means making repairs to objects that can be salvaged, sewing your favourite jeans with a patch or even finding creative ways to cut apart and reuse furniture (see the Crate Furniture project, on page 30)!

This book uses materials that were available in local thrift shops and sometimes even just found in the street – being a sustainable maker means looking at the possibilities of the materials around you and getting inspired by their properties and potential.

Audrey Love, 2021

Project
01.
Printing
with nature

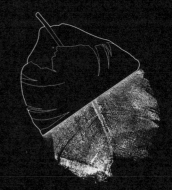

Junk shops often have a great selection of home goods. For this project, I found some nice curtains – and the $5 price tag made them hard to ignore. Inspiration struck with this printmaking technique. This project shows you how to add a bit of colour and pattern to your fabrics using no more than some pigment paint and leafy garden waste!

Tools & Materials

Tools:

- Small paintbrush
- Foam paintbrush or rubber roller (I used a Brayer)
- Old towel
- Drill (with drill bit and screwdriver head)

Materials:

- Pair of curtains
- Selection of leaves
- Acrylic paint (in colours of your choice)
- Acrylic medium
- Glass palette or glass picture frame
- Curtain hardware (I used a curtain-rod kit)

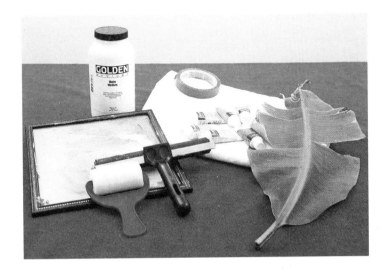

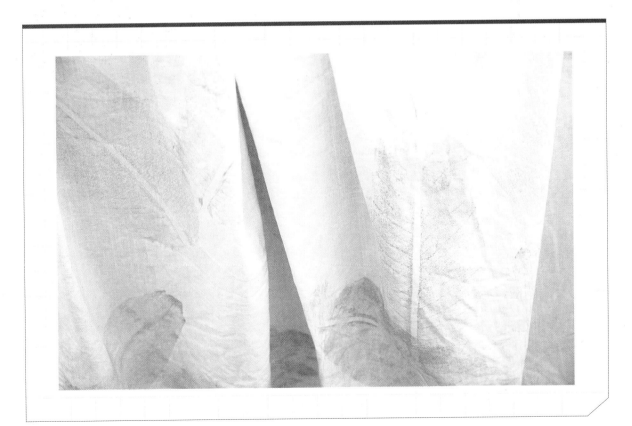

Step 1:
Laundering the fabric

Since I bought these curtains second-hand, I decided that they could do with a wash before painting. If you purchase brand-new curtains, then laundering them will also remove any added starches, which can prevent the acrylic paint forming a lasting bond with the fabric.

If the fabric comes out of the wash looking wrinkly, it may be a good idea to press or steam it before applying pigment to the surface of the curtain.

Step 2:
Sourcing plant material – aka printing blocks

I'm lucky enough to live in Los Angeles, a location where so many incredible plants are able to grow, and so I didn't have to look far to source the leaves I used. The banana leaf and bird-of-paradise leaf (shown here) both came from my front garden.

I selected leaves that were quite broad and which had natural splits in them, so I taped these together on one side to prevent them separating any further. This also made the leaves easier to coat with paint in the next step.

Step 3: Preparing paint

To create the stamp ink that is applied to the fabric, do not work with the acrylic paint straight out of the tube. This paint is physically denser and has a lot of pigment, meaning it takes a long time to dry and can be more vibrant than you wanted. To avoid this, simply add an acrylic medium to dilute the paint.

I chose to work with a matt fluid medium, which has a very fast drying time and thins pigment beautifully, leaving a consistency almost like washing-up liquid, flowing and spreading easily. I used a small paintbrush to mix the paint and medium.

This may be a matter of preference, but mixing paint on a glass palette makes it really easy to incorporate all of the acrylic medium and pigment. On paper or cardboard, the paint and medium are likely to be only partially absorbed.

Step 4:
Coating the leaves

Using a foam paintbrush or rubber roller, coat the top side of the leaf with a very thin layer of paint. It should look like translucent pigment on the leaf. If you want a print with more of the details from the leaves, and less of a bold outline, try flipping the leaf over and printing with the underside. If you use a regular bristle brush, instead of a foam paintbrush or roller, you may get a bold outline and less detail, but a more vibrant saturated colour. Play with it – painting is meant to be fun!

Step 5:
Stamping

Place an old towel or slightly squishy material under the fabric you're printing to protect your work surface from any paint bleed-through. Now it's time to start stamping. Once your leaf is coated with medium and pigment, gently flip the leaf over and press it into the fabric. Carefully move the foam paintbrush/roller over the back of the leaf to ensure all the paint is transferred to the fabric. Repeat with other leaves in different colours. Leave to dry for at least 15 minutes before moving. Soak the paint off all the plant material before adding to a compost bin.

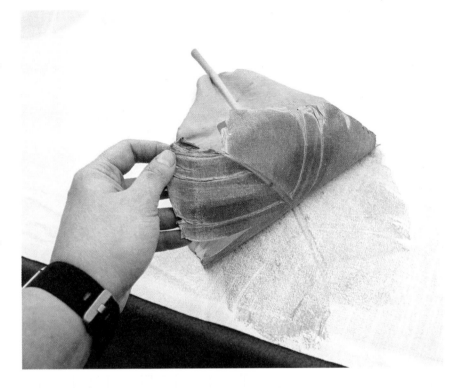

Step 6:
Hanging and caring for curtains

Using the drill and your choice of curtain hardware – here, I used a curtain-rod kit – hang your newly decorated curtains at a window.

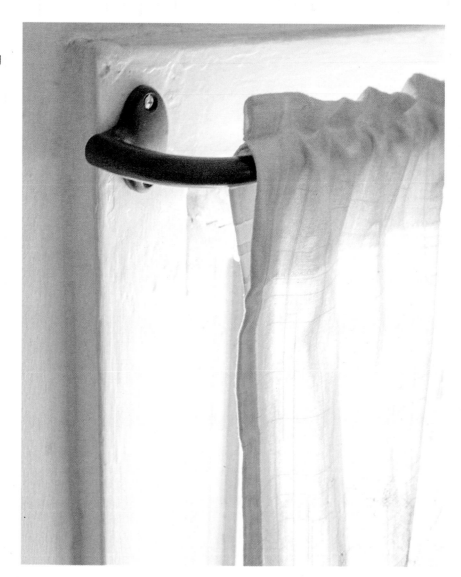

↙

Tip:

If the curtains ever
become too dusty,
the acrylic paint
is washable! Just
throw the curtains
into the washing
machine on a cold
setting and allow to
air-dry.

Project
02.
Cyanotype chair reupholstery

This easy introduction to learning upholstery techniques starts by reupholstering a simple chair. Reupholstering is a sustainable choice, consuming fewer resources than new furniture and minimizing landfill waste. This project shows you how to dye natural fabrics with the light-sensitive cyanotype process, which is a great way to mask stains on tattered fabrics.

Tools & Materials

Tools:

- Screwdriver or drill (to dismantle the furniture item)
- Sanding block (optional)
- Nitrile gloves
- Fabric scissors
- Large glass bowls (do not use steel tools or bowls, as this material can affect the cyanotype sensitizer)
- Large sink
- Staple gun (if your furniture piece has a wooden base)

Materials:

- Furniture item such as a chair that could use a little love
- Alcohol-based cleaner/spray paint (with primer) or brush-on house paint/spray-on clear acrylic (all optional)
- 1 m (3 ft) sturdy natural fabric (such as cotton, denim, silk or bamboo)
- Mattress foam or padding for the seat (optional)
- Cyanotype kit (containing ferric ammonium citrate and potassium ferricyanide)
- Leaves, plants or other flat objects (I used thrifted doilies to create these lace-like prints)
- Masking or marking tape (optional)

Step 1: Get ready

The first step when reupholstering is to plan how you're going to restore your chair. Typically, the steps are to disassemble the furniture into component pieces, assess what needs to be repaired, make all the necessary repairs, and then recover the piece with a new textile. Whatever alterations your piece requires, it's important to keep track of your steps so you can work backwards to reassemble your retrofitted furniture.

If the wood or metal frame of your furniture item is in good shape, it may not need to be sanded or painted. If you'd like to change the colour of your piece of furniture, you can use a sanding block to even out any chipped paint spots, then re-coat using a spray paint with primer or some brush-on house paint.

The folding chair I used quickly came apart by removing just four screws, but the chair you're working with may require a drill to come apart more easily.

After the chair was in pieces, I used a sanding block to clean up small patches in the enamel coating on the back of the chair, and then I cleaned the whole chair with an alcohol-based cleaner. The spray paint I used specifically had primer in the formula, and, once the blue paint was completely cured, I coated each chair with two layers of spray-on clear acrylic.

Step 2:
Copying the seat pattern

Using the original vinyl seat cover as template, I cut a piece of heavyweight cotton denim, leaving a little room on all sides as a seam allowance. It's much easier to cut away any extra fabric later than it is to wish it was still there!

Whatever piece of furniture you are reupholstering, you may also need to replace the foam or padding of the seat. You can find these items at most craft shops. Check out the crate bench in this book for tips on working with foam (see page 30).

I ended up cutting a new piece of batting for this chair. Batting isn't as thick as foam. It is easier to cut and can be layered if desired. It also conveniently creates a non-absorbent surface for the fabric dye to dry on in the next step.

Tip:

Always check out the bedding and textiles section of local thrift shops. Sometimes you can find great raw materials in bulk that just need a wash to be used for your next sewing project. This white brushed denim had a few yellow stains that I didn't worry about, since I knew it was going to be dyed – it was available at a super-low price.

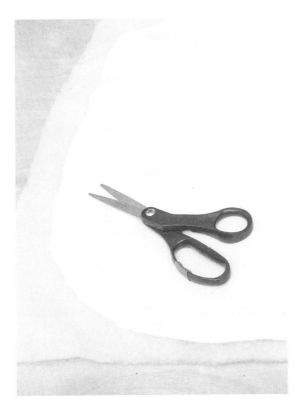

Step 3:
Making cyanotypes

It's time to dye the fabric using light-sensitive cyanotype chemistry. Follow the instructions on the cyanotype kit to hydrate your chemistry at least 24 hours before using.

Most kits are mixed in a 1:1 ratio of ferric ammonium citrate to potassium ferricyanide. It's best to use non-porous, glass mixing containers or, alternatively, you can use recycled takeaway containers to mix the chemistry in. Make sure you wear nitrile gloves while mixing and coating the fabric.

When the chemistry is mixed, most people prefer to use a brush or spray bottle to apply the mixture to the fabric, but I like to pour a little bit at a time over the fabric in a glass bowl and wring the chemistry though the textile. It creates a more textured and dreamy-looking finish.

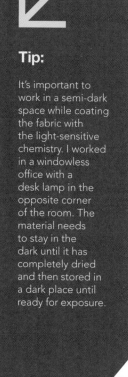

Tip:

It's important to work in a semi-dark space while coating the fabric with the light-sensitive chemistry. I worked in a windowless office with a desk lamp in the opposite corner of the room. The material needs to stay in the dark until it has completely dried and then stored in a dark place until ready for exposure.

Step 4: Exposing your printed fabric

Once the fabric is completely dry, it will be a slightly teal-y yellow and ready for exposure to sunlight. You must complete this step outside or in a well-ventilated area.

Place the fabric on a piece of backing board, such as a flattened cardboard box, and begin creating your contact print. Lots of people like working with natural items like fern leaves or pressed flowers to create fun outlines on the fabric, but you can really get creative. Any relatively flat object that can leave an interesting mark works well: keys, rope, paper cut-outs, etc. I'm particularly fond of using lace and doilies.

After you've finalized your design, carry the light-sensitive fabric on its rigid support out from the dark space you've been working in and place it in the sun. Exposure time will vary anywhere from 30 minutes to 1 hour, depending on the brightness of the sun and the thickness of your fabric. You'll be able to tell when the exposure is complete as the colour will become a teal-y blue and the parts in the shadows of your print will still look slightly yellowish.

You may want to test this process on smaller swatches of fabric to get the hang of it first before coating and exposing your final pieces.

Tip:

If you're using items that have some height, or are super lightweight like a leaf with an arch in its stem, consider using a pane of glass or sheet of acrylic over your print to keep your items flat while they're being exposed – this could even prevent them from blowing off your print if it's windy outside.

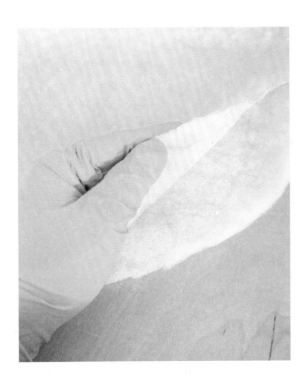

Step 5: Fixing your print

....

When the exposure is completed, bring everything back into the dark space and remove all of the items that you placed on the fabric. Wearing gloves, immediately rinse the fabric with cool water in the sink. Keep running water through the fabric until there is no more greenish water coming out.

Before moving on to the next step, make sure the fabric is completely dry. Do not hang it in the sun to dry. Instead, lay it flat on a towel out of direct sunlight or hang it in a dark cupboard. For an extra layer of durability and fabric protection, you can spray the print with a layer or two of spray-on acrylic clear coating.

Step 6: Replacing the fabric seat on the chair

For the chair I was restoring, there were no staples or adhesives holding the fabric in place. Instead, the fabric is squeezed between a pressure-fitted metal ring that forms the bottom of the seat. In positioning the fabric, I was careful to feature some of the prettier parts of the doilies on the fabric and cut away the parts with slightly blurred edges.

This printing process is great fun and can be used on all kinds of natural textiles to create one-of-a-kind customized items. The possibilities are endless! Have fun looking for furniture pieces to restore – how you found the item can be just as exciting as giving the piece a new look.

Tip:

If your seat pad is made from wood, you can use a staple gun to attach your fabric by wrapping the top of the seat with the dyed fabric and then turning the seat over to staple down the edges to the wooden underside. Don't be afraid to use a lot of staples and pull the fabric taut before driving each staple into the wood. Any excess fabric that is left over after stapling can easily be cut away with a sharp razor blade.

Project
03.
Crate
furniture

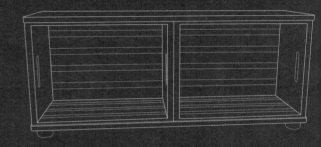

This great project is made from material that was saved from landfill. I sourced this set of crates from a post on Craigslist: a local shop no longer needed a display and was going to discard them. Not only do crates get a new lease of life in this project, but so do old foam mattresses. Learn here how to carve up foam for seating projects.

Tools & Materials

Tools:

- Tape measure
- Sander
- Clamps
- Drill
- Circular saw
- Paintbrushes

Materials:

- 2 × boards (to match the size of the top and bottom of the bench)
- Sanding discs
- Acrylic sealant (glue)
- Metal fasteners
- Furniture feet
- Latex paint
- Brush-on clear acrylic (optional)
- Mattress foam, batting or reupholstery fabric (optional)

Step 1: Designing a bench

Start by working out which sides of the crates you'd like to join together – connecting the longer sides will create a taller bench profile. For this project, I chose to bond the sides of the bench that were structurally the strongest. This created a bench that was about 90 cm (36 in) long, 31 cm (12½ in) high and 24 cm (9½ in) deep.

Tip:

Craigslist allows you to set up email alerts for categories such as "Free in your city", and you can further refine your search by postcode and key words. If you're patient, then this approach can really pay off!

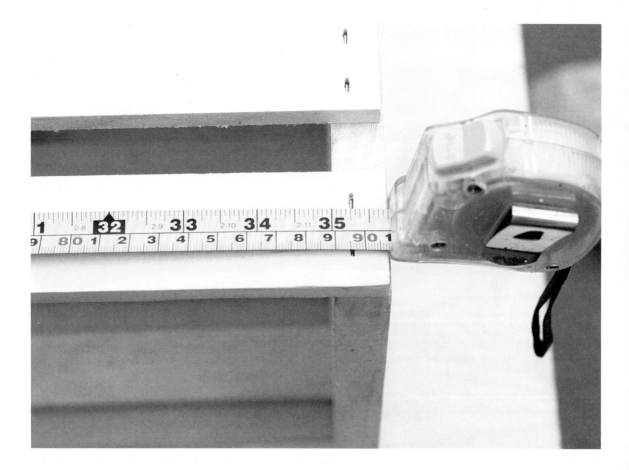

Step 2: Woodworking

A reliable way to create lasting wooden furniture is to use both glue and metal fasteners. After the crates are thoroughly sanded, apply glue to both sides of the wooden faces you're bonding, clamp them together, then screw in your metal fasteners. Allow the glue to set for at least 30 minutes. Once the glue is completely set, use a circular saw to cut down a piece of plywood or board to create the top and bottom of the bench which is 5 mm (¼ in) bigger than the dimensions of the crates on all sides. Using wood glue with MDF can cause the MDF to warp and swell with moisture – here it's best to just use fasteners. Make sure you pre-drill, or the material will split. Add four furniture feet to each corner of the bench.

Tip:

Don't want your screw heads showing? Use a countersink drill bit before screwing in your hardware to create a flush surface. For a sleek finish, backfill the screw heads with stainable wood filler to completely cover your hardware.

Step 3:
Finishing

When the structure is complete, it's time to paint! MDF is unsightly, but it paints up nicely. If you want to sand the MDF to a smooth finish before painting, make sure you wear safety goggles and a mask – it's important not to breathe in the particulate.

For the bench shown here, I used two coats of a lustre-finish latex house paint, followed by two coats of acrylic finish, all applied with a synthetic bristle paintbrush to avoid bubbling.

Step 4: Making a cushion

If a foam mattress has lost its support, you can give it a second life by repurposing the foam for furniture. What is more, it's fun to cut up foam. There are specialist foam-cutting tools available if you're looking for precision, but most people agree that the best way to cut foam is with an electric carving knife – the kind you'd use for a Sunday roast.

I cut a thin strip off the end of the mattress, and then carved the piece into three segments that could be re-attached with spray adhesive. To bond foam, spray both bonding faces with adhesive and allow to tack for 2–3 minutes before joining the two pieces. Complete your bond by squishing the foam faces together, then allow at least 30 minutes to cure completely.

Put a thin layer of batting on top of the foam pieces to hide any seams that are showing, then wrap the cushion in upholstery fabric. There are lots of techniques for making cushions, but since I wanted something washable in case our dog spoils it, I made a Velcro closure for the underside.

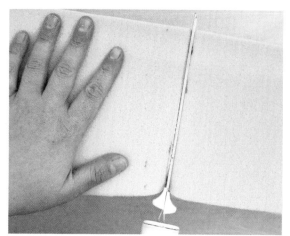

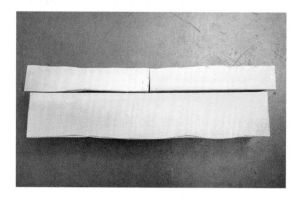

Tip:

Always use a straight stitch when you are sewing Velcro; zigzag stitches can get stuck in the hooks and jam your sewing machine.

Explore available materials

This project used wooden crates, but it could just as easily be made from plastic milk crates. If you decide to use plastic crates, consider using lag bolts and fender washers in the existing holes of the crate to compress them together rather than screwing the crates together side by side. It's worth exploring the fastener aisle of the hardware shop to get inspiration for your own interpretation of this bench.

Project
04.
Upcycling
fast furniture

In a city, there are often "street scores". I once found
some boards and drawers, used here and for the
Crate Furniture (see page 30). The Earth will thank
you for upcycling too. Modern furniture often uses
chipboard and medium-density fibreboard (MDF),
which contain harmful chemicals that can leach and
contaminate groundwater. Upcycling helps!

Tools & Materials

Tools:

- Drill
- Circular saw
- Sanding tools
- Tape measure
- Clamps
- Nitrile gloves
- Syringe (optional)
- Silicone brush
- Mixing sticks and resin cup
- Heat gun or torch (optional)

Materials:

- Boards from old drawers or wooden pallets, or an existing table
- Table legs and hardware
- Two-part Epoxy resin
- Heat-transfer edge banding trim
- Decorations (I used pressed flowers)

Step 1: Prepping timber

When working with upcycled wood or boards, you'll want to get them to a blank state first. Remove all metal fasteners and cut the boards down so there are no undesired holes or grooves in the wood, and then sand all sides. If you have access to nice woodworking tools, such as a jointer or planer, you may also want to run the wood through those too because furniture boards are often warped.

Measure the materials and then cut them to the desired size using the circular saw.

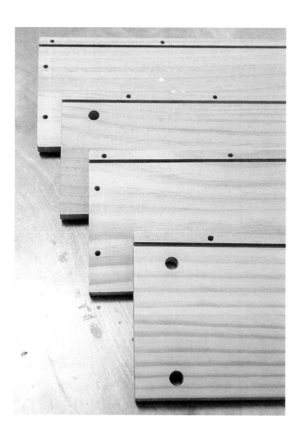

Step 2: Make a table

If you're working with an existing table, feel free to skip this step.

Glue the boards together and clamp them in place. For extra support, you can add crossbeams to the underside of the table, using glue and the drill to screw in the nails. Sand all surfaces and round the edges with a router or sander.

To prevent resin seepage later on, apply a thin line of epoxy resin between the grooves of the boards and allow to cure completely.

I like using a syringe to do this because its precise application cuts down on sanding after the adhesive has dried, but a small silicone brush can work just as well.

Once the small amount of resin has set, flip the table over and attach the legs. After your table is assembled, it's time for one last pass with a sander.

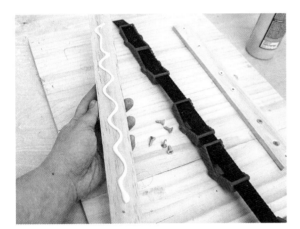

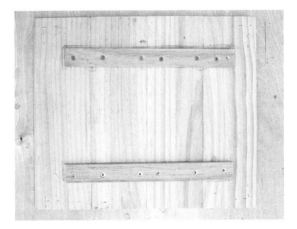

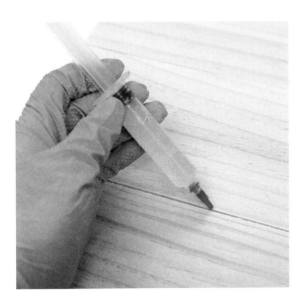

To prevent resin from spilling over the sides in the next steps, apply a heat-transfer edge banding trim with an iron. Encase the edges completely. Leave extra space between the table and the top edge of the banding trim for the resin.

For my table, I decided to embed dried flowers in resin. The flowers were very brittle, so I positioned them carefully with a pair of tweezers.

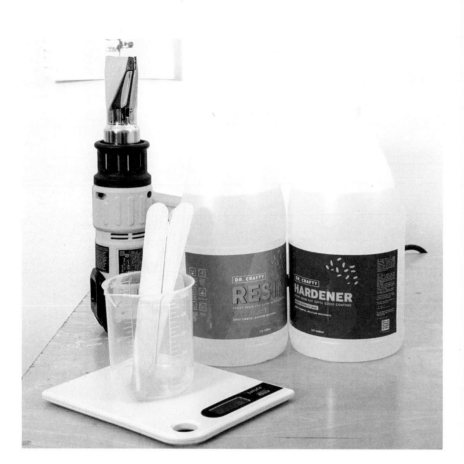

Tip:

It's important to mix the resin in small batches to extend its work time. The chemical reaction is exothermic – which means it creates heat. When the heat cannot escape the resin and hardener mixture, it builds up, and the epoxy cures even faster. By working with small amounts of resin in thin layers and with lots of airflow over the surface area, we're able to control how fast the table cures, giving us a long time to set our flowers and remove any bubbles.

Step 3:
Measuring the resin

Measure the resin in a jug with a scale or in a graduated mixing cup. Mix the resin thoroughly for at least a minute, making sure you scrape the bottom and sides frequently. If you're measuring by weight, you need to measure 100 parts resin to 84 parts hardener.

Step 4:
Starting your pour

Pour the resin around the table edges in thin streams from high above the flowers, or your choice of keepsakes, and allow to spread slowly.

Apply the resin in batches until the table is covered completely. Leave to set for 24 hours. If you're allowing the resin to set in a dusty space like a garage, cover your piece with a clean plastic sheet – I make a little tent out of rubbish bags and tape. You will be tempted to poke and check the resin, but it's best just to forget about the piece for at least a day, depending on the resin you're using, as, counter-intuitively, thinner layers of resin take much longer to cure.

Tip:

If you see a few bubbles building up in the resin, pop them with a pin. If you see a lot of bubbles building up, they are likely not going to be solved with a pin, but a blow torch or heat gun works really well for popping bubbles in resin.

Step 5:
Finishing touches

Cut away the excess trim at the top of the table and sand down the entire surface, creating a soft chamfer around the leading edge. Go over the the surface of the table with a sander and 120-grit sandpaper. This should leave the resin looking "frosty". This ensures the tabletop has a more uniform appearance and removes any surface defects from the previous layer.

Mix another batch of resin and brush this over the top of the table using the silicone brush. Leave to set, as before.

Voila! A beautiful keepsake that you've customized and successfully kept out of landfill. This furniture will last for ages and offer a reminder of the ethos behind living sustainably.

Project
05.
Paper and plaster lamp

I keep a small stash of old newspapers around my studio because they are so useful to have when you're making a mess, or need some packing material in a pinch, or even need to make a first draft of a paper template. For this project, old newsprint is used in a much more classic craft application, with a twist!

Tools & Materials

Tools:

- Mixing containers (recycled food containers are great for this)
- Scissors
- Paintbrush
- Sandpaper
- Nitrile gloves

Materials:

- Small inflatable exercise ball
- Packing or masking tape
- Castor oil
- Old newspaper or scrap paper bags
- Wood glue
- Casting material (such as reinforced plaster)
- Acrylic paint and acrylic medium (optional)
- Lamp hardware

Step 1: Preparing the form

Using a small exercise ball as a base form, inflate the ball to a firmness that springs back when you touch it, but doesn't feel like it's going to pop. To protect the ball from being destroyed by wood glue, start by wrapping it completely in tape, making sure you don't block the inflation port. The papier mâché glue in this project is a PVA glue, so rub the form with a thin layer of castor oil first, to prevent the glue from sticking to the tape.

Tip:

Castor oil is a skin-friendly mould release that can help when casting and forming with any material.

Step 2:
Get ready

Begin by cutting out newsprint strips and squares. The strips will be used to cover the sides of the lampshade and the squares will be used to reinforce the top where the hardware is attached.

Mix 1 part water to 3 parts glue. Protect your work surface with scrap paper as you are working with watery glue (which can get messy). Waterproof wood glue is particularly good because it bonds extremely well and even a thin coating is very strong.

Step 3:
Applying the paper

Dip a paintbrush in the water-and-glue mixture and coat one side of a cut square of newsprint. Apply the square to the top of the base form, then coat the top of the square with another coat of the glue mixture. Repeat over and over again, overlapping the pieces of newsprint and using the squares at the top and the strips on the sides, until you have coated the entire form with paper, then allow to cure overnight. Once dry, rub lightly with sandpaper.

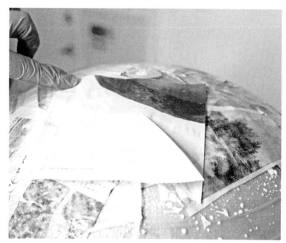

Step 4:
Applying the plaster

Repeat the previous step, but instead of using wood glue, use a thin mixture of casting plaster. It is usually recommended that you mix 3 parts plaster to 1 part water, but for this project, I recommend that you use 1 part plaster to 1 part water, and stir the mixture frequently between paper applications. Allow the plaster to cure completely overnight.

Once the plaster has cured, wear a pair of gloves to mix another batch of plaster (again at a ratio of 1 part plaster to 1 part water) and texturize the outside by dipping your hands in the mixture and applying it to the outside of the lamp. This helps shore up the outside and prevent it from flexing when the ball is deflated. Let this final coat cure for at least 24 hours.

Tip:

It's very important to wear gloves when you are handling plaster, as it can damage your skin and gets hot when setting.

Step 5: Deflate and paint

Carefully remove the pin of the exercise ball, allowing it to deflate slowly without applying any pressure.

After about 20 minutes, you should be able to remove the ball easily from the inside of the lamp's opening. The leading edge at the bottom of the lamp will probably need to be cleaned up with a pair of scissors.

If you like the look of the white lamp, you can skip the painting stage, but consider painting the inside with a metallic spray paint so that it better reflects the light emitted from the bulb.

Acrylic paint is ideal for painting the outside of the lampshade, but the colours are too opaque and I didn't want to lose the look of the textured plaster. To thin the colour and get a more watery application, I mixed the opaque acrylic paint with acrylic medium, which is basically clear "paint". I just used a rough chip brush to apply the paint, but the opportunities for getting creative on the outside are endless.

Step 6:
Bright idea

I found a lamp kit that made it easy to screw the lampshade to the lamp hardware. The lightbulb port is threaded through the hole at the top of the shade and a locking nut secures it in place from the other side. Just add a light bulb, and voilà, it's a lamp!

Hang the light from the ceiling using a hook and enjoy an illuminating object that you created yourself!

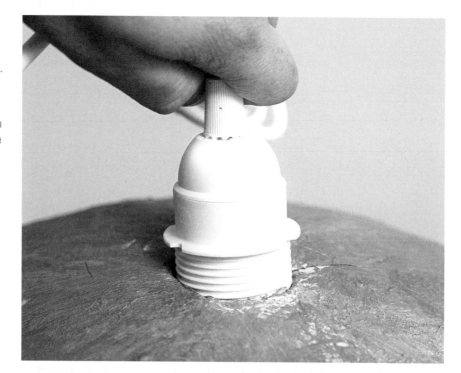

Project
06.
Hanging gutter planter

In my town, there is a reclaimed builders' supply warehouse which has great deals on used bits from building sites. Suppliers like this are a great place to get ideas for incorporating used materials around your home. While here, I saw some awkward lengths of gutter, and went online to find the right end caps. Once I had all the parts, I headed to the hardware shop to pick up the rest of my materials.

Tools & Materials

Tools:

- Tape measure
- Permanent marker
- Speed square
- 2 × bar clamps or a mitre box
- Hacksaw
- Drill and drill bits
- 2 × pairs of pliers
- Level

Materials:

- 3 × 60 cm (24 in) lengths of vinyl gutter
- 6 × end caps (to fit the profile of the gutter)
- 6 m (20 ft) chain
- 12 × No.8 38-mm (1½-inch) bolts
- 24 × No.8 fender washers
- 12 × No.8 lock washers
- 12 × No.8 nuts
- Hanging brackets (I used a compression bar and S-hooks so I wouldn't damage the outside walls of my building, but this project could be easily anchored with any hooks able to support at least 12 kg/25 lb)

Step 1: Marking and cutting

Mark out three sections, each 60 cm (24 in) long, on the vinyl gutter using a permanent marker and a speed square. A speed square is highly recommended because the perpendicular edge of the square can catch on the slippery gutter, making it easier to draw your cut line.

After all of the gutter has been marked up, cut the required lengths using a hacksaw. Vinyl gutter can be slippery on any surface, so make sure you clamp it down in at least two places before attempting any cuts or drilling any holes.

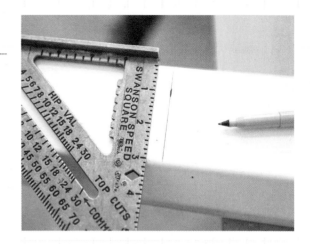

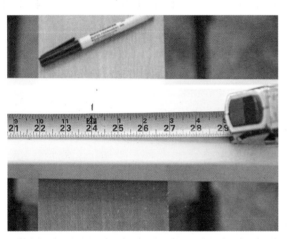

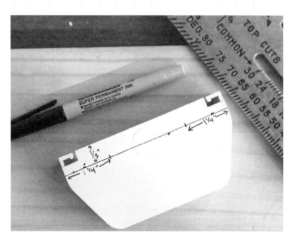

Step 2: Drilling holes

Drill holes in the bottom of the lengths of gutter for drainage. Too many holes, and the potting mix can dry out too quickly, and not enough holes means your plants' roots may rot. I spaced the holes about 7.5 cm (3 in) apart, in an X-shape, all along the base of the gutter.

The mounting holes on each of the planter's end caps require a bit more precision. The holes in the caps need to be evenly spaced and at exactly the same height on each piece. Depending on the profile of the gutter, make sure you mark the holes above the horizontal centre line to prevent the planter tipping once it is hanging up.

Attaching the end caps to the lengths of gutter is a breeze: they just slide on and are held in place with a built-in rubber gasket.

Step 3: Adding hardware

Cut four lengths of chain. The length of chain you use will vary depending on what you'd like to plant and where you want to hang your planters. Cutting chain is a great way to ruin a pair of wire snips, so instead, I used two pairs of pliers to gently bend the chain open and closed.

The pictured lengths are 1.25 m (40 in) long, with 40 cm (16 in) spacing in between each length of gutter.

This chain is flat, and has a large opening, which means it is easy to pass a bolt through the link that will be secured to the end cap. Each link is sandwiched between two large fender washers to prevent slipping.

The order of the hardware on the bolt should be: washer, chain, washer, through the end cap, lock washer, nut. While two fender washers around the chain may hold it in place, it also allows it to move and sway. The pressure washer on the inside of the cap holds everything in place.

Tip:

When watering these planters, I start at the top and work down, so that the water can flow from the top gutter to the ones hanging below.

Step 4:
Hanging and planting

Hang your empty planter and check that it is level. Half-fill the planter with potting mix before planting your seedlings, or fill completely with potting mix and then add seeds. I chose herbs, lettuce and spring onions.

Project
07.
Wine crate
greenhouse

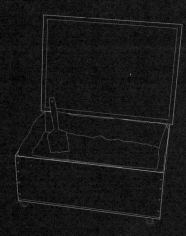

This is a great space-saving way to start a herb garden. Turn a poster frame and a wine crate into a moveable greenhouse which can be used all year round. The poster frame here has an acrylic sheet, making it ideal for outdoors, but if you use a glass frame, add some rubber bumpers to the corners to prevent shattering.

Tools & Materials

Tools:

- Drill and drill bit
- Staple gun and staples (for outdoor use)
- Nitrile gloves

Materials:

- Wine crate
- Landscaping fabric
- Castor wheels
- Poster frame (the same size as the crate)
- Hinges
- Two-part epoxy resin
- Silicone sealant (optional)

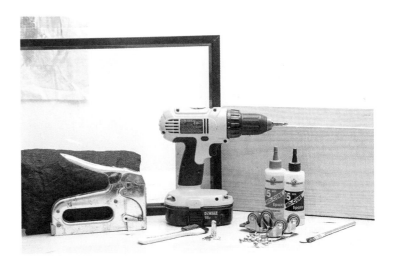

Step 1:
Get ready

Wine crates are often made from young timber that has been dried or cured quickly, which can cause the boards to warp. This makes crates perfect for outdoor use and gardening, but it also means you have to make sure the boards will hold up. Sometimes they need a bit of wood glue, epoxy or extra fasteners before the crate is ready for its day in the sun.

After inspecting your crate and shoring up any joints, flip it over and drill some drainage holes. Space the holes evenly. Depending on the size of crate, you'll need between 10–20 holes to retain the right level of moisture in the potting mix.

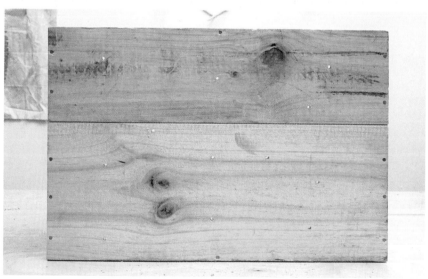

Step 2: Making the planter box

Lining the crate with landscaping fabric helps with water retention in the soil bed and also adds longevity to the life of the crate outdoors. Depending on your climate, this may not be necessary, but I live in a place with very low humidity and want to support the seedlings' growth with as much water as possible.

Landscaping fabric is easy to cut and work with. Measure out a length that will completely line your crate. It is OK if there is extra cloth; this can be tucked in when it is stapled to the edge of the crate.

Using a staple gun with staples rated for outdoor use, staple the landscaping fabric to the edges of the crate. Do not staple within 3 cm (1 in) of the corners, which is where the hinges will be attached.

Once you have lined the crate, flip it back over to drill the holes and screws for your castors. Adding wheels to the planter means you never have to pick it up to move it to a sunny spot. It should be noted that the castors shown here have two locking wheels, which are handy for keeping the planter in place on uneven ground.

Step 3:
Adding the hinges

....

Depending on your poster frame, you may need a different type of hinge than the one shown here. The frame I worked with was fairly small, so I used heavy-duty jewellery box hinges.

Using a pencil, mark out where you'd like the holes for your hinges to go. Set your hinges aside and pre-drill or pre-screw all the holes for the hinges before you try to attach the frame to the wine crate. This ensures you're not having to make new holes while holding a wobbly hinge in place.

After pre-drilling, mount your hinge to the frame first, then the crate. It may be a good idea to go back over the hinges with a bit of epoxy on the frame side to prevent tear-out as the wood ages in the sun.

Tip:

When shopping for hinges, make sure you read the whole package. They often have a weight rating, which is important when suspending heavy frames. Also check that the hinges come with the recommended nails or screws.

Step 4: Extra weatherproofing

This step is optional, but it will definitely extend the life of your miniature greenhouse. Silicone sealant is great for outdoor projects because, like epoxy, it lasts a long time, but is potentially removable if something needs to be repaired. Silicone can't be used for a weight-holding bond, but it's perfect for adding a seal to the top of the greenhouse.

With the acrylic back in place in the frame, cut off the tip of the tube of silicone and put on some nitrile gloves. Run a bead of sealant around the edge of the whole frame. With your fingertip at an angle of 45 degrees, swipe along the edge to even out the seal. Remove the excess silicone by wiping your finger on a rag as the sealant builds up. Allow to cure for at least 24 hours before moving outside.

Step 5: Starting your garden

I live in a dry climate and conditions never dip below freezing. With this in mind, I used two layers of potting mix. The first layer of potting mix is about 3 cm (1 in) thick and rich in composted bark that will retain moisture for longer. The second layer of potting mix is 4 cm (1½ in) thick and made from perlite and coir, which is lightweight to allow roots to form and easily nourish the germinating seeds with lots of air.

Tip:

You can start any kinds of seedlings in your miniature greenhouse. Just make sure you follow the instructions for your climate on the back of the seed packet. Happy growing!

Step 6: Fill with seeds

After the bed has been filled with a seedling potting mix, lightly water the greenhouse bed. Gently create rows in the damp potting mix with the tip of your finger and sprinkle 3–5 seeds in each little divot. For the size of wine crate pictured here, I'm using half a packet of lettuce seeds.

The germination success and growth rate will vary depending on what time of year it is, and how much sun your garden gets. Keep in mind that if it rains, no water is getting into this seedling patch, so check on the moisture levels of your greenhouse often.

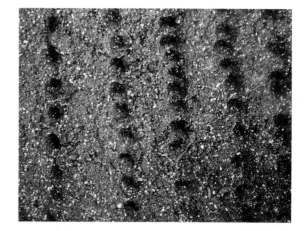

Checking on your plants

Be mindful of the temperature inside your greenhouse. If it is getting too humid or warm, prop open the unhinged edge of the frame slightly.

Don't pluck the lettuce seedlings until they are at least 5 cm (2 in) tall. This gives the plants a chance to become established, but allows for thinning before new growth is overly congested.

When plants are ready to be thinned out, take a pair of scissors that have been recently swabbed to avoid contamination, and cut away small growth from the base of the plant. These are perfect microgreens for salads, but they do tend to wilt quickly.

Project

08.

Self-watering Planters

This project shows you how to take an old water bottle and milk carton and use them to create a self-watering planter made from concrete. It's so fun to get clever when it comes to making concrete moulds! Anything that's watertight can be turned into a mould, even single-use food containers.

Tools & Materials

Tools:

- Razor blade
- Permanent marker
- Scissors
- Foldback clips
- Nitrile gloves
- Particulate-filtering dust mask
- Safety glasses
- Mixing cup
- Silicone spatula or other mixing tool
- Hammer or palm sander
- Drill and masonry bits
- Sanding block

Materials:

- Milk carton
- Plastic food container or water bottle
- Vinyl/duct tape and masking tape
- Baking parchment
- Castor oil
- Cement mix
- Wick cord

Step 1: Get ready

Start by cleaning the milk carton and then cut off the top so that you're left with a boxy form. This will be the base of your mould. A smaller food container like a yogurt cup or water bottle is perfect for creating the inside shape of your planter.

I used a water bottle with a ridged texture on the outside, but I knew this would be hard to remove from the concrete once it had set. To make the bottle more uniform, I wrapped it in vinyl tape (as shown). Using smooth tape like this is a great way to change the surface of your form without having to bust out a lot of extra tools and materials.

Step 2: Prepping the mould

Cut the corners of the milk carton with a razor blade so that the carton opens out into an X-shape. This will make it easier to remove the planter from the mould after the concrete has cured.

If you are planning to reuse the mould, line it with baking parchment. Duplicate the shape of the box on more baking parchment using a permanent marker and scissors. Fold the paper to mimic the shape of the carton, and seal the edges with vinyl/duct tape.

Place the water bottle – or whatever food container you are using – inside the empty mould and mark where it bottoms out. Then lift it up about 2–3 cm (¾–1 in) and make another mark; this will create the bottom of the planter and water-catch.

Coat the mould and baking parchment with castor oil, which is a natural alternative to chemical mould release. Tape around the edges of the carton, and place the paper back in the form, clipping the top of the paper to the edge of the carton.

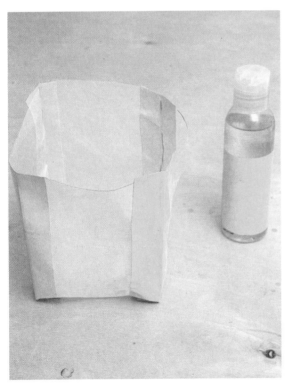

Step 3: Casting the planter

It's important to think of safety when you are working with concrete. You definitely don't want to breathe in this stuff or get any in your eyes. Wear gloves, a mask and some eye protection.

Open the container of concrete and measure out about 500 ml (2 cups) of cement mix. Using a mixing tool, slowly incorporate small amounts of water into the mix, stirring to break up any clumps, until you have the consistency of a clumpy pudding.

Gently tip the wet cement mixture into the mould. Slowly press the water bottle/food container into the cement until the mixture starts creeping up the sides of the carton. Depress the bottle into the cement until the edge on the outside of the carton lines up with the lower mark you made on the bottle.

Use a hammer or palm sander (without any sandpaper in it) to vibrate the mould and knock out any bubbles. Secure the water bottle/food container into place with some tape so that it doesn't lift up, then set aside to cure for 72 hours.

Repeat steps 1–3 to make a second form – this will become the water reservoir for the planter.

Tip:

As long as there is not too much water in the concrete, the concrete will set after 3–4 hours. The difference between set concrete and cured concrete is easy to recognize. Set concrete is dark grey and will feel damp to the touch, while cured concrete is a much lighter grey and has a dustier feel. You can speed up the curing time by removing the exterior mould after it has set, but I recommend letting the interior form remain in place until the concrete has completely cured.

Step 4: What to do if your concrete breaks

The concrete sometimes breaks while it is being removed from the mould. Don't worry, all is not lost. I got impatient here and tried to remove the water bottle from the inside of one of the casts before it was completely cured and it split in two. Glue to the rescue!

If this happens, apply a thick layer of all-purpose construction adhesive to the crack and then bond the planter back together. This glue needs a full day to cure, so it's a good idea to tape your form up while the glue finishes setting.

Step 5:
Adding watering wicks

Watering wicks are awesome for planters; it means you have to water less often and your plants won't suffer from under- or over-watering. To add the wicks to the planter, pick one of the cast concrete shapes and drill holes using a masonry bit along the edges of the basin inside the form.

Cut 15-cm (6-in) lengths of wick cord and gently burn each end to extend the life of the wick. Tie a loose knot and thread the end through the bottom of the basin with the knot resting at the corner.

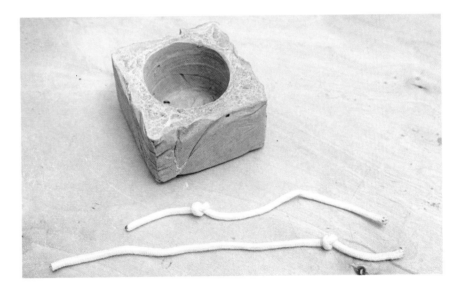

Step 6: Enjoy!

Before filling your planter, take a sanding block to the concrete and smooth down any rough or uneven edges.

This planter is great for succulents or small seedlings that you'd like to keep an eye on.

Fill the bottom basin of your planter with water, then gently dip the wicking ends into the reservoir. What are you going to do with all that time now that you're watering your garden less?

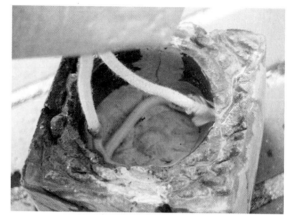

Project
09.
Solar lamps

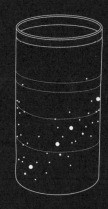

Sometimes holiday snacks and cookies come in fun reusable steel or aluminium tins that are great for repurposing. This project uses old food tins to create pretty and sustainable back-garden lighting that's powered by the sun. This project involves eating cookies, in case you were looking for another reason to start work on it soon.

Tools & Materials

Tools:

- Scissors
- Permanent marker
- Gloves and safety glasses
- Centre punch or drill
- Sanding block
- Soldering iron (depending on the solar light)

Materials:

- Upcycled metal food container or tin
- Steel foil tape
- Solar jar light
- Silicone sealant
- Galvanized metal wire

Step 1:
Clean up the outside

First things first, make sure you have eaten all the snacks that came in your tin. Thoroughly clean the tin and wrap it in steel foil tape. Steel tape is a bit more expensive, but it holds up well against the elements and reinforces the tin or container along its glued seam.

After applying the tape, take a burnishing tool or a dry rag to the outside of the tin to press out any wrinkles that may have shown up in the tape. I like the look of the burnished wrinkles; the texture makes the lamp look more handmade.

Tip:

Ripping stainless steel or any foil tape will often leave a jagged edge. If you want an aesthetically pleasing edge, it's best to use a pair of scissors.

Step 2: Customize the lantern

Decide what design you want on your tin – mark this out by dotting permanent marker in your desired shape.

It's important to wear safety glasses for this next stage because tiny flakes of metal can go flying in every direction, and that is not a fun trip to the hospital.

Using a centre punch or a drill, start drilling holes in the tin. If you make fun shapes or patterns, the light will project through the holes in the same pattern. I tried to mimic a galaxy around the side of the tin and punched a heart in the bottom.

After you've finished drilling your design, punch a larger hole on each side of the tin, about 4 cm (1½ in) down from the lip, so that a hanging wire can be threaded through the opening later.

To avoid getting cut by the lantern's sharp metal edges, it's a good idea to run over the outside with a sanding block.

Step 3: Time for electronics

Sand both the top and bottom of the lid of the container, then drill a hole in the centre.

The solar lights shown here are designed for the tops of mason jars and are easy to disassemble and repurpose. On top there is a small solar panel and the underside of the jar twists apart to reveal the circuit board and rechargeable battery.

There is a thin set of red and black wires that run from the solar panel to the circuit board. These must be disconnected, then threaded through the lid of the tin and reconnected to the board. Make sure you mark which wire is positive (red) and which one is negative (black).

To weatherproof the electronics, run a bead of silicone sealant along the inside edge of the plastic edges of the solar lamp, taking care to avoid the circuit board and wires. Press the silicone-covered edge into the top and bottom of the tin's lid, and secure with clamps to cure for 24 hours.

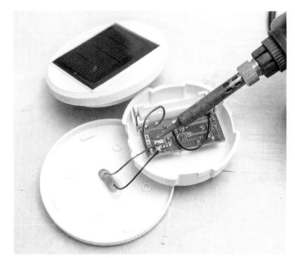

Tip:

It's important to keep your soldering tip in good shape. Keep steel wool nearby to clean it while it's hot, and use alcohol to clean your wire leads and solder joints before you apply any flux and solder.

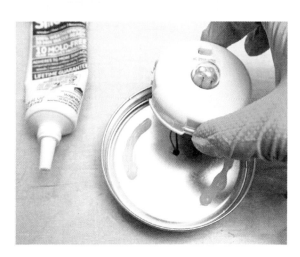

Step 4:
Hanging your lamp

Cut the desired length of galvanized metal wire to create a hanger for your lantern. Thread the wire through the top two holes you made previously below the lip of the tin.

Hang the lantern in your garden or put it on an outdoor table.

Allow the lantern to charge in the sun for at least a day. The lights automatically turn on after the sun sets; it's pretty clever! The batteries on these particular solar lamps were quite large and stay illuminated throughout the night. A smaller, coin-cell battery may not stay on until sunrise.

Project

10.

Ladybird house

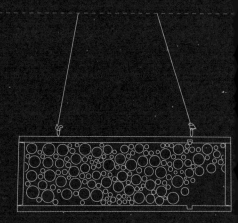

Ladybirds can really help with pest control in your garden, eating mites, aphids and other insects that damage your plants. They also act as pollinators, so give back by building them a home! You can build a little wooden box, or look for one in a junk shop or flea market. For this project, I used a single-bottle wine box to make a spacious ladybird house.

Tools & Materials

Tools:

- Saw (a bandsaw, ideally, or shop for short segments of bamboo)
- Resin mixing cup
- Mixing stick
- Sandpaper
- Drill and eye bolts (optional)

Materials:

- Wooden box
- Bamboo pieces or lengths
- Masking tape
- Two-part epoxy resin
- Wood sealant (rated for outdoor use)
- Hardware for hanging (eye bolts work well)

Step 1:
Cutting the bamboo

I found bamboo lengths with both a wide and narrow diameter at my local nursery.

Using the depth of your box as a guide, cut down each length of bamboo so that it is a bit shorter than this. My box was 11.5 cm (4½ in) deep, and I cut each length down to 10 cm (4 in).

Dry-fit the bamboo as you go, leaving a gap at the edge of the box for adding cotton pads or leaves once the house is outside.

Tip:

Bamboo lengths can be cut using a hacksaw, but it's best to cut them with a power tool such as a bandsaw, to work with the circular shape of the bamboo.

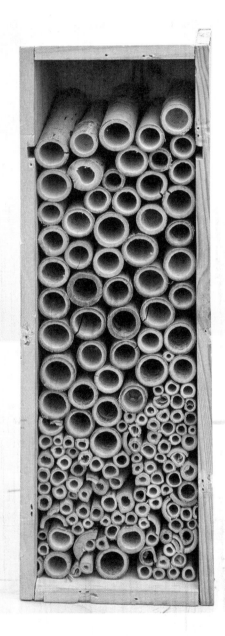

Step 2:
Gluing pieces

Once you're satisfied with how many pieces you've cut, tape any gaps in the bottom of the box with masking tape to prevent glue from leaking out the sides during gluing.

Traditional wood glue only bonds to the exposed fibres of bamboo. This project necessitates bonding to the smooth, end-grain of the bamboo, so it's best to use an adhesive like epoxy or, in this case, polyester casting resin.

After mixing about 100 g (3½ oz) of adhesive (using 50 g/1¾ oz of resin and 45 g/1½ oz of hardener), pour the mixture into the box. Flood the box with adhesive across the entire bottom, working it into the corners with the mixing stick. One by one, and working from a corner, begin to set bamboo pieces individually in the box so that they are standing vertically.

Allow the adhesive to cure for 24 hours before moving.

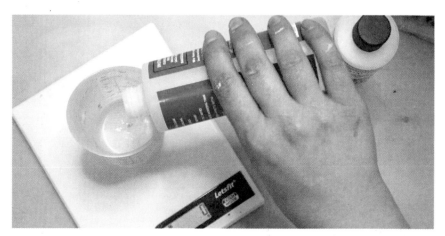

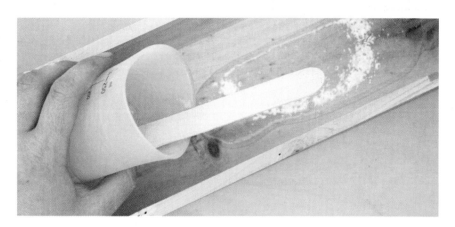

Step 3:
Finishing touches

Once everything has completely dried, gently sand the exterior of the box, and coat with a wood sealant that's designed for outdoor use.

If you'd like to hang your ladybird house, drill holes and add eye bolts to the sides. If you'd like to mount it on a post, consider using a piece of rebar and hanger tape to make a stake-able pole that you can move around your garden.

Step 4: Releasing your ladybirds

Ladybirds aren't very active at night while in cooler temperatures. So, if you release them at night, they have a higher chance of adapting to their new home while they are "sleepy".

Have a meal ready for them when they wake up! Watering the plants around the outside of your house will create many watering stations for your new neighbours, and if you don't have a visible number of aphids in your back garden, insert a couple of raisins in the bamboo slots for the ladybirds to feed on.

I will note that ladybirds were surprisingly hard to find in my town! The cashier at my local nursery recommended ordering them online. A few Internet searches later, I was able to find an abundance of ladybirds available for delivery to our garden. They arrived promptly along with a note on the package to store them in the fridge and to release them within three days.

Project
11.
Tablet sleeve
from a sweater

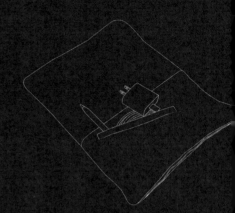

Having purchased a new tablet that came with
a small stylus and a power cord, I knew that
both were easy to lose. I was in the market for
a protective sleeve or caddy, but shop-bought
options were expensive -- so I made my own! This
project is made from a zip hoodie that had been
lying around ever since I got red paint on it.

Tools & Materials

Tools:

- Cutting mat
- Seam ripper
- Paper guide
- Straight edge or ruler
- Scissors or rotary trimmer
- Pins
- Sewing machine

Materials:

- Old zip hoodie or sweater
- Sewing thread

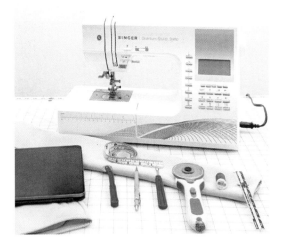

Tip:

Don't throw out old clothes! If they are still in good shape, see if you can donate old clothing to a shelter or charity. Or take to organizations that work with rag manufacturers to recycle unsold items and keep fabric out of landfills for longer.

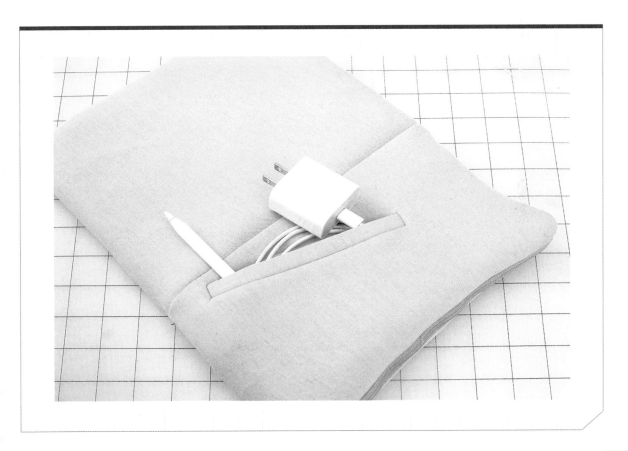

Step 1:
Getting started

Buying zips at the craft shop can be expensive, so why not just use the one that's already in the hoodie or sweater you're working with? Using the sharp end of a seam ripper, and with the clothing zipped up, gently pull out the stitches that are holding it in place, being careful not to rip the fabric attached to the zip.

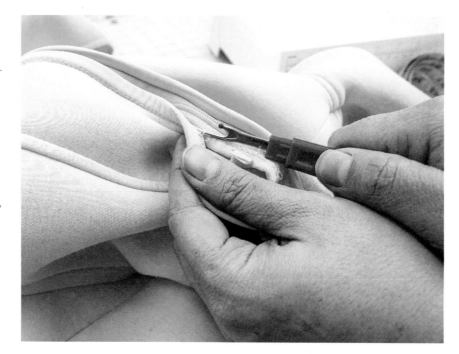

Step 2:
Create a template

I made a paper guide to figure out how big my fabric rectangle needed to be to accommodate my tablet, with a little bit of wiggle room to get it in and out of the opening. Add about 1cm (½ in) to all sides for a seam allowance.

Step 3:
Making the most of your remaining fabric

Once the zip is removed, start sizing down your remaining fabric. Create a long strip of fabric by cutting the hoodie/sweater in two, cropping it at the armpits. The best way to do this is with a straight edge and a rotary trimmer. You can press the edges of the ruler into the armpits and then use it as a guide to make your cut.

Lastly, I removed all patterned edges (such as ribbed cuffs) to make it easier to run the fabric through the sewing machine. For this particular hoodie, I was left with two pocket panels and one back panel. Using the machine, sew the fabric back into one long strip, pressing each of the seams after they have been stitched.

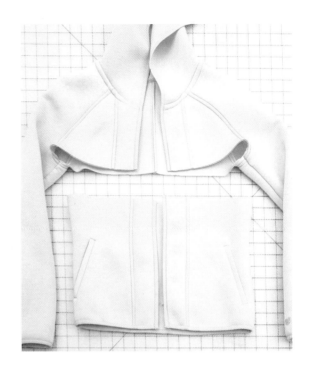

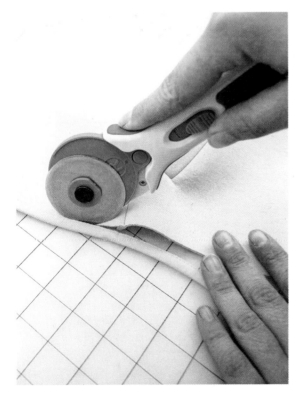

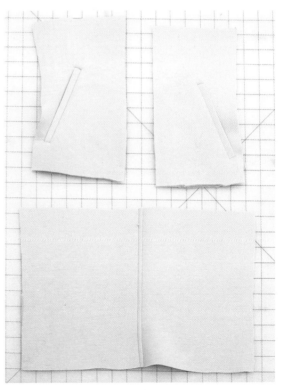

Step 4:
Adding a zip

Pin the zip to the edges of the pocket panels so that the right sides are touching, and the pockets are facing out.

Your sewing machine should have a zip presser foot. This foot holds the zip teeth in place while the needle is driven into the fabric part of the zip, instead of through the teeth.

Stitch the zip into place. What remains is a loop of fabric that is a little bit bigger than the size of your tablet.

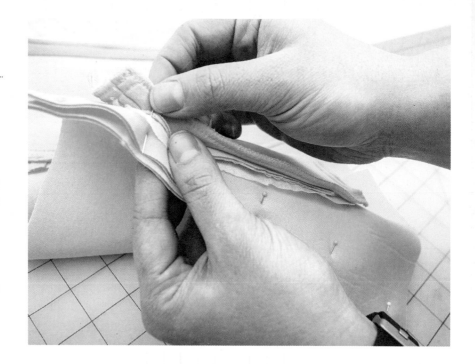

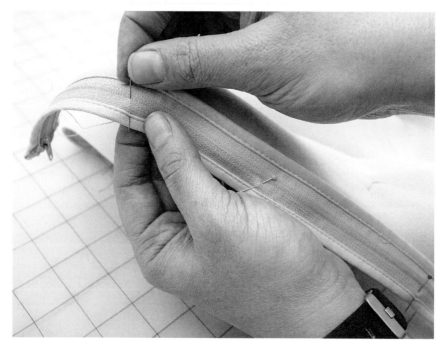

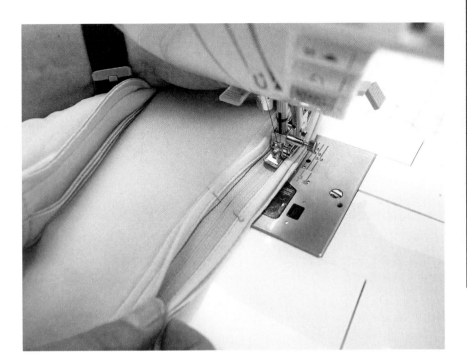

Tip:

Consider how this zip is going to be used while you are placing it. I lined up the edges so that I didn't have to worry about the zip being stopped by the fabric corner of the tablet sleeve.

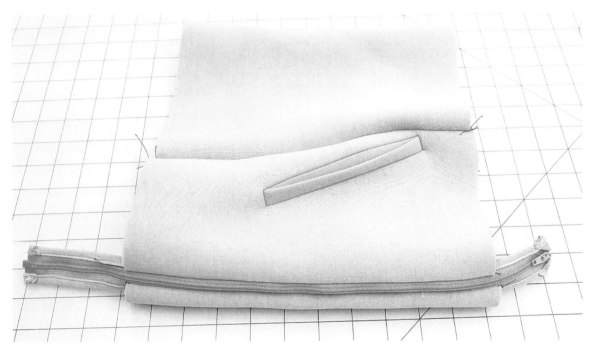

Step 5: Finish stitching

Finish sewing the rest of the edges of the tablet sleeve. Depending on the fabric, you may want to use an overlock stitch to prevent fraying.

The finished sleeve is perfect! It protects the screen of my tablet and conveniently stores the accessories in the pockets, while the bright colour makes it hard to lose in a room or on a messy workbench.

Project
12.
Insulated lunch bag

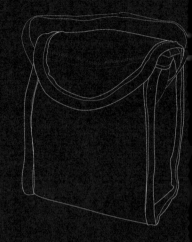

This project uses unconventional materials such as Tyvek®, a hydrophobic textile, and Mylar insulators, which are used by frozen food distributors. Tyvek® is a soft, waterproof synthetic fabric, which means it cleans up easily and nothing sticks. The Mylar-coated, dry-ice bag adds insulation, but you could also use insulation fabric or an old towel.

Tools & Materials

Tools:

- Cutting mat
- Scissors, razor blade or rotary trimmer
- Sewing machine (with a leather needle)

Materials:

- Tyvek® envelopes
- Packing tape
- Food-safe insulation material (such as Mylar)
- Bias tape
- Sew-on snaps

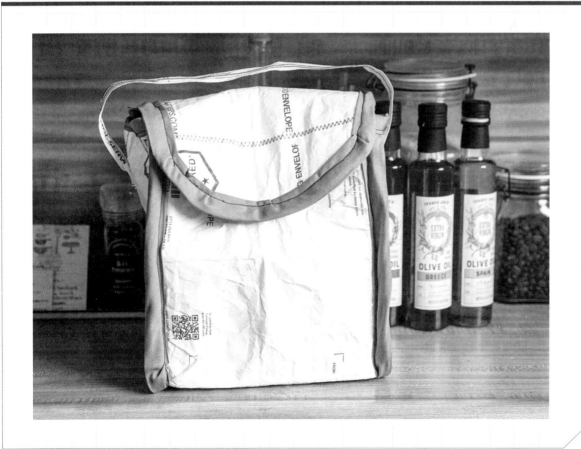

Step 1: Prepping the envelopes

Tyvek® envelopes have some flaps and folds that are too difficult to sew around, so it's best to cut off all the sides as well as the sticky adhesive strip. Once those are cut away, you will be left with two rectangular panels from each envelope. Attach the short end of each panel together with some packing tape.

For this lunch bag, I used four envelopes to create two long strips by stitching three panels together. Use a zigzag stitch on the sewing machine to create one long, smooth, continuous rectangle of fabric.

Check the picture for patterning suggestions. You can make this lunch bag whatever size you'd like, but keep in mind that you should have a seam allowance of 1 cm (½ in) around all edges.

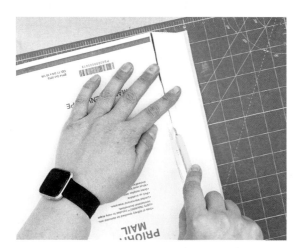 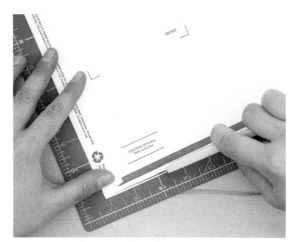

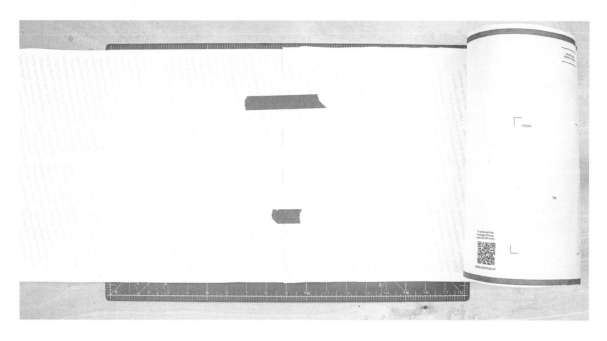

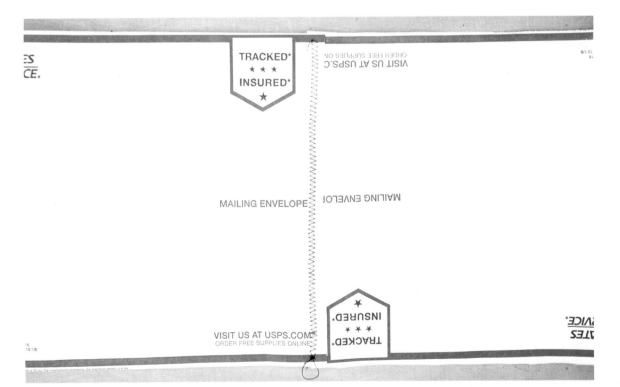

Step 2: Sewing the pieces

Sandwich your insulation fabric between the two strips of exterior lunch bag material. Make sure there is at least 2.5 cm (1 in) on all sides of the insulation fabric, so that it isn't sewn into the edge seams of the material when the lunch bag is finished with bias tape.

The lunch bag gets its shape from sewing folding seams in four places perpendicular to the longest side of fabric. I gave my flap a curved top, cutting away the insulation fabric to sweep the same line as the top curve, with 2.5 cm (1 in) of space in between. This could be any shape you want, but a flap will definitely help keep your items cold.

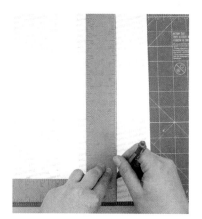

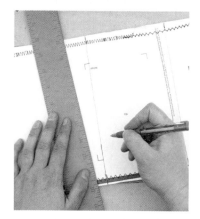

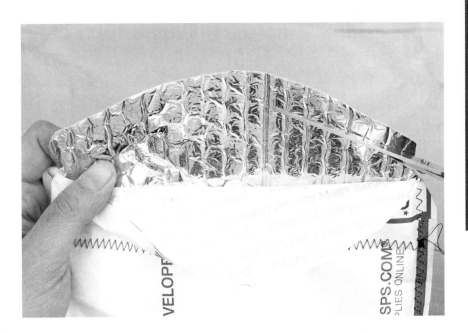

Tip:

Using a leather needle when stitching Tyvek® will help you to puncture the fabric more easily and also prevent the needle from jamming in the sewing machine.

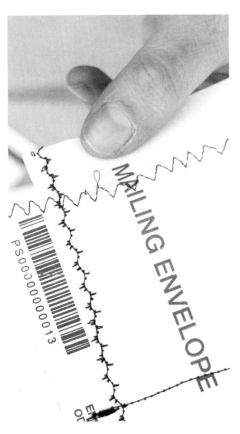

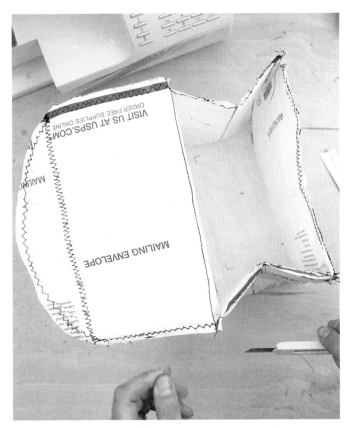

Step 3: Getting it all together

Once the folding seams have been added, and all of the edges are bonded, it's time to add the sides. You can create collapsible sides by running a seam up the centre of each panel – a straight stitch is best for this fold. To prevent the fabric from jamming in the sewing machine, notch the corners where the bottom of your bag will connect to the side panels.

Once the sides are attached, it's time to add the bias tape. The bias tape will help cover all the previous stitches and also reinforce the outer corners of the lunch bag. If you wish, you can also create a handle from an off-cut scrap of fabric and tack it down to the side panels of the bag.

I decided to add a simple snap closure, hand-sewing it on, but you could add a buckle or even use Velcro instead.

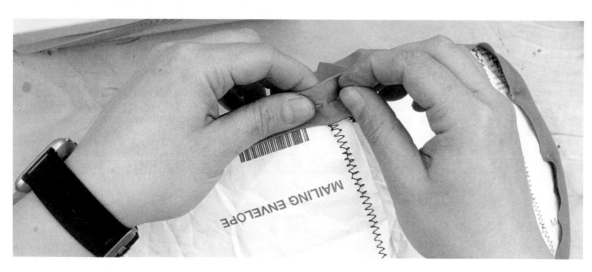

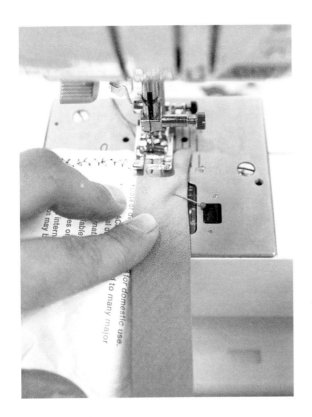

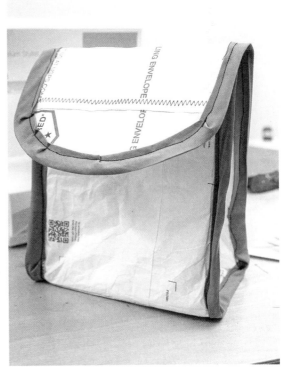

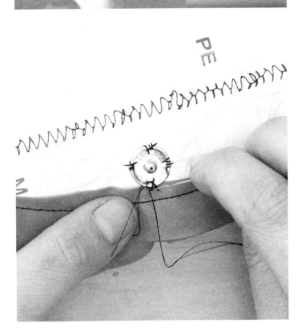

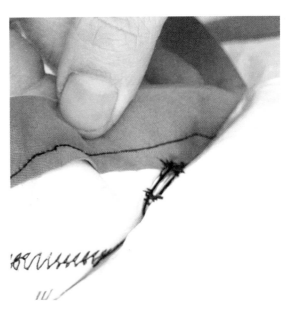

Explore more options

Making a lunch bag is a great way to challenge yourself at your sewing machine, and a great way to use up pieces of scrap fabric. Practise your sewing skills and make creative sustainable gifts for all your friends – they'll happily think of you whenever they reach for their midday snack and see your awesome creation.

Project
13.
Upcycled
radio

Household electronics like audio players and TVs suffer from a high turnover. However, with a basic knowledge of electronics, you can upcycle a classic gizmo into a modern digital device. Give your used electronics a second life by harvesting their internal components to make customized projects like this handy Bluetooth radio.

Tools & Materials

Tools:

- Precision screwdriver set
- Small metal snips
- Pliers
- Drill
- Rotary tool
- Soldering iron

Materials:

- Vintage radio or speaker
- 5–12 V rechargeable battery kit
- Bluetooth receiver
- Small 5–12 V amplifier kit
- Small, full-range speakers
- Standard rocker DPST (Double Pole Single Throw) switch
- Double-sided foam tape or hot glue gun
- Solder wick

Step 1: Planning your circuit

When fixing up old electronics with new modern components, it's important to be mindful of three things: power, circuit design and size.

The first step to building a portable speaker is thinking about how loud you want it to be. This will inform how much power you require and indicate how big the battery needs to be. A small, 5-V, 300-milliamp battery will power a quiet speaker, which is perfect for a small toy or instrument, while a 12-V, 3-amp battery is loud enough to be heard over a group of about 10 people.

If you're a beginner, don't worry about circuit design. There are so many cool options for pre-made amplifier kits that will teach you the basics of

electronics. If you're looking to design your own circuit, make sure that all of your components are compatible. So, if you find a rechargeable battery pack that outputs 12 V, look for an amplifier circuit that will run at 12 V. Connect a 12-V battery to an amplifier rated only for 9 V of current, and you will toast your circuit.

As for size constraints, you can only go as big as the enclosure you want to use, so make sure all of your components will fit inside your casing. When you're researching your parts, look for the data sheet in the product description. This will give you the dimensions of the component part, as well as indicate the operating voltage and the provide the wiring information.

Step 2: Prepping the enclosure

The vintage speaker enclosure needs to be disassembled and retrofitted to fit the new Bluetooth audio circuit.

Most old electronics can be taken apart with the help of a precision screwdriver, handheld snips and pliers. These are all the tools an aspiring tinkerer needs to get started.

This project uses a rotary tool with a cut-off wheel to chop down the screws holding the broken speaker in the amplifier. The space is needed to contain the large battery pack in the next step.

Lastly, this radio's enclosure needs two holes – one for the power switch and one for the amplifier's combination power and volume knob. Making the hole with a drill is easy, but cutting out square shapes in panelling can be tricky. To cut rectangles in your enclosure, carve out the shape using both a drill and rotary tool. Start by drilling four small holes in the corners of your panel cut, and then drill one large hole in the centre where your rectangle will need to be. Go back through with the rotary tool and connect the dots using a mini cut-off wheel, flap wheel or other engraving head. Test-fit your switch as you go to see if you need to clean up the edges.

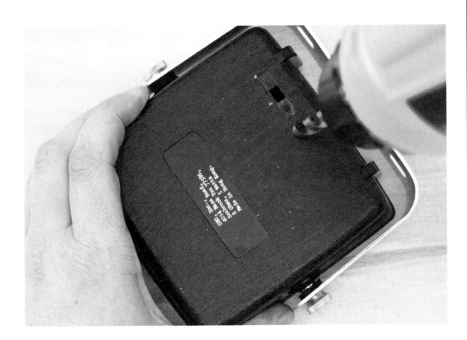

Tip:

If you're using a rotary tool to cut plastic, it's important to use the correct personal protective equipment (PPE). The material heats up and can release gas, so make sure you're wearing safety glasses and an R95 particulate-filtering mask – you don't want to be breathing in any vapours or dust.

Step 3: Building the circuit

For this upgraded radio, I based the circuit on a 12-V rechargeable battery module. There was a spot in the battery module to wire in a power switch, but the power pack you use may be different, so be sure to check the circuit diagram included with the battery. From the battery pack, I connected a 12-V amplifier module and a Bluetooth audio receiver.

The 12-V amplifier module had a volume knob already connected to its circuit board, so the only connections that had to be made besides power were audio input and output. For audio input, wire a cable from the amplifier to the Bluetooth receiver, and for output, connect the full-range speakers to the amplifier circuit module. Be sure to check out the diagram for more information on how current flows in this circuit.

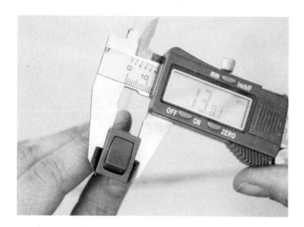
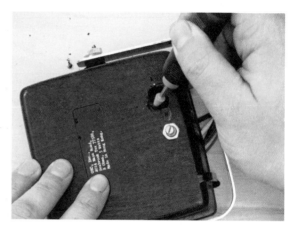

Map Your
Circuit

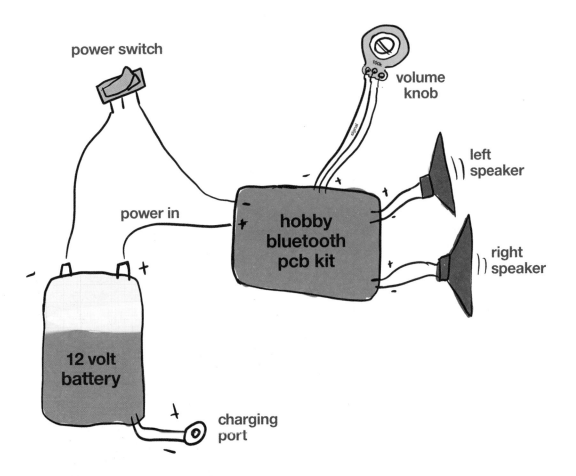

power switch

volume
knob

100k

signal

power in

hobby
bluetooth
pcb kit

left
speaker

right
speaker

12 volt
battery

charging
port

Step 4:
Getting it all together

If components are not screwed down, double-sided foam tape can be used in most electronics to keep them in place – it isn't conductive, is super sticky and even shock-absorbing. It took a few iterations to figure out how to get all the pieces to fit in the Bluetooth radio, but I was able to sandwich all the components together and anchor them with tape. Lastly, I taped down the speakers so that the speaker cones were pointed through the metal mesh screen.

I carefully squeezed the screen back into place and the radio was ready for use. This battery is rated for at least 24 hours of playback, so it will be a while until I have to open it up to charge again, but you could just as easily add a recharging port for your project.

The last detail was adding a knob cover for the volume dial on the back of the radio. I used a brushed aluminium knob that matched the brushed aluminium handle.

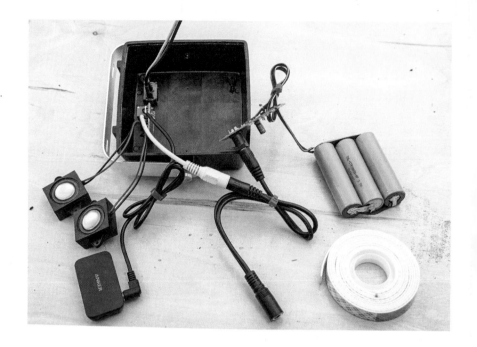

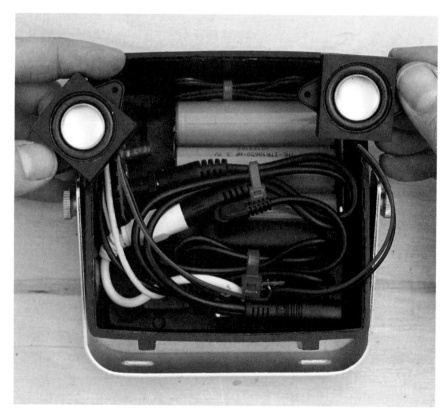

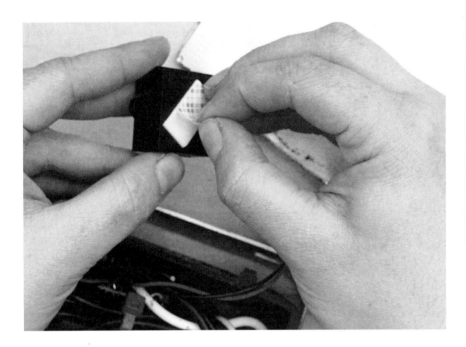

Tip:

Fancy jazzing up the colour of your radio? There are many cool knob colours available so don't be afraid to play around with your aesthetic.

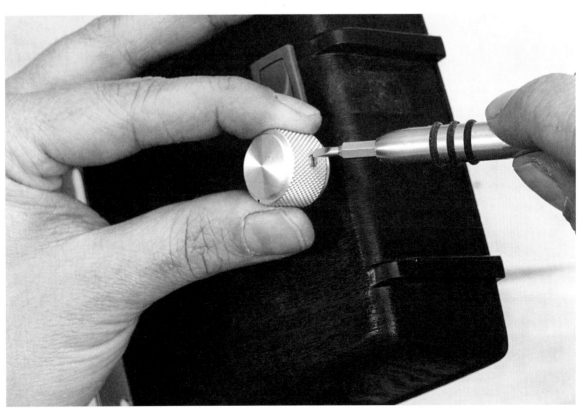

Trying to get rid of old electronics?

Perhaps you're not one for tinkering, but you know your device is still reusable – well, there is a huge community of people out there who may be interested in your broken vintage electronics! Spare these antiques from heading to the skip and consider listing your item on eBay or a similar site. Are your ageing electronics beyond repair and so obsolete that no one may be interested anymore? Your city probably has a way to help you donate your e-waste responsibly. Check your local government website on the best way to recycle your ageing electronics and keep your city a green place to live.

Project

14.

Shampoo and conditioner bars

I first learned that you could make your
own shampoo bars when I was planning a
backpacking trip. I realized that solid shampoo is
perfect for travelling because it will never spill in
your bag and it isn't packaged in a plastic bottle
that will need to be recycled later. A double win
for sustainability and functionality!

Tools & Materials

Tools:

- Empty water bottles or a pre-made silicone mould
- Double boiler (or use a saucepan and glass bowl)
- Razor blade or knife
- Spray bottle with rubbing alcohol
- Airtight container (for storing the soap bars)

Materials:

- 450 g (1 lb) oatmeal melt-and-pour soap base
- 8 g (1 tsp) mango butter
- 30 g (2 tbsp) castor oil
- 1 g (20 drops) rosemary essential oil
- 1 g (20 drops) grapefruit essential oil
- 1 g (20 drops) cedarwood essential oil
- 3 g (1 heaped tbsp) dried nettle leaves
- 5 g (1 handful) dried hibiscus flowers (not ground)

Tip:

This soap is designed to work on all hair types, but you can add different oils and herbs depending on your hair type. Nettle, rosemary and hibiscus all support hair growth at the scalp, while the castor oil and mango butter both nourish the strands of hair.

Step 1:
Prepping the moulds

Note: The ingredients for this soap have been listed by volume and weight. I recommend that you weigh everything out: I've tried to make these soap bars by volume measurement, but the results are not as predictable and the cure time is sometimes longer. The soap base used in this project is a ready-made mix of oil, fats and sodium hydroxide (also known as lye), which can be melted and blended with other botanicals and herbs. (All true soaps contain lye, but this way we don't have to handle or mix it.) If you're interested in making soap from scratch without using a pre-made soap base, invest in some personal safety equipment and read up on the dangers of mixing sodium hydroxide. Making your own soap base is more cost-effective than the method detailed here, but also potentially more hazardous and time-consuming.

If you are using a pre-made mould, feel free to skip this step. If you have plastic bottles or food containers in your recycling bin, it's a great way to repurpose them into a mould. The plastic bottles used in this project were tapered. If you're working with a tapered shape, make sure you cut it below the widest point of the container so that the soap is easy to free once it has cured in the mould.

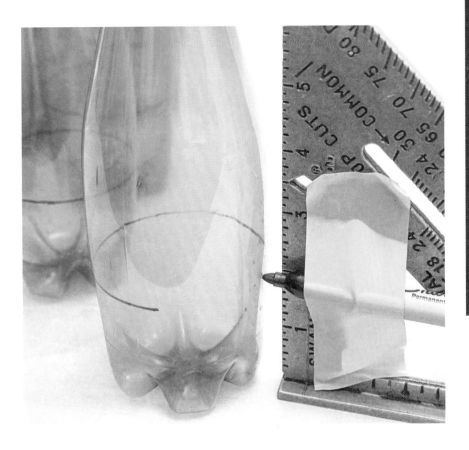

Tip:

If you need to make a mark around a cylindrical object, tape a permanent marker to the edge of a ruler, then spin the work piece. The marker will leave a perfectly straight line as you rotate the cylinder.

Step 2: Making the soap

Turn on the double boiler, or place the glass bowl over a saucepan of water and heat to a gentle simmer; a rolling boil could cause your soap to burn.

Cut the soap base into chunks with a razor blade or knife. It should be very easy to cut, like cutting into cold butter. Add the soap base and oil ingredients to the double boiler or bowl. Begin melting the ingredients down, making sure your heat stays low.

Stir the bowl occasionally to mix all of the oils with the base. Once all the ingredients in the bowl have melted completely, gently stir in the nettle leaves and hibiscus flowers until they are completely incorporated. Keep stirring occasionally for 10 more minutes. The hibiscus adds a bit of colour to the base; other herbs or flowers may also gently dye your soap, but they shouldn't stain your hair.

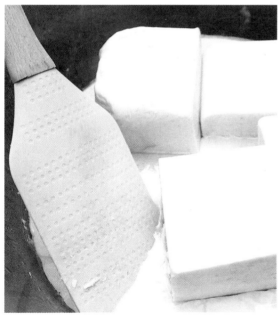

Step 3: Casting into moulds

Gently spray the moulds with rubbing alcohol, then carefully pour the warm melted mixture into your moulds.

Spray the top of the soap with rubbing alcohol, which prevents air bubbles and makes the soap shiny when it is cured. The soaps pictured here were allowed to set in their moulds for 15 minutes before a little more dried hibiscus was sprinkled on top, and then they were set aside to cool for several hours.

Soap will be completely cool and firm to the touch when it is ready to be turned out of the mould. If the soap gets stuck in the upcycled plastic mould, try taking a hammer and carefully tapping on the bottom of the container.

↙

Tip:

Make more bars
than you can
use in a year?
These shampoos
also make great
gifts! Why not
experiment
with different
repurposed
materials for gift
wrap, or even make
your own gift box
altogether?

Step 4: Tips for using and storing

If you have short hair, try rubbing this shampoo bar in your hands to create a lather, then massage the suds into your scalp and hair.

If you have long, luxurious locks, you may want to wash your lengths less often. To keep your scalp clean, wet your hair and scalp, then tie your hair back into a loose ponytail. Take the wet soap bar and massage across the scalp in strokes from front to back. Set the bar aside and then massage the soap into a lather on the scalp without sudsing up the lengths. Remove the hair tie and rinse as normal. The shampoo will run through the lengths of the hair, gently cleansing the strands without stripping the hair.

Store the cured soap in an airtight container; these bars should be good for up to a year.

Project
15.
Reusable bulk
food bags

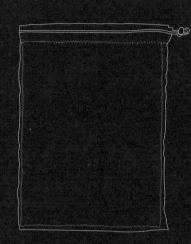

I love shopping at farmers' markets, but am
frustrated by how often these businesses rely on
single-use plastic bags. This project uses lightweight
nylon – perfect for produce because synthetic
materials resist staining. T-shirts are also great to
upcycle, but natural fibres can rot, so make sure you
store only dry goods such as nuts and rice.

Tools & Materials

Tools:

- Fabric tape measure
- Iron
- Fabric scissors
- Fabric marker or tailor's chalk
- Pins and a pincushion or pin magnet
- Sewing machine
- Seam gauge (optional)

Materials:

- Lightweight fabric
- Sewing thread
- Cord or thin rope
- Cord stoppers

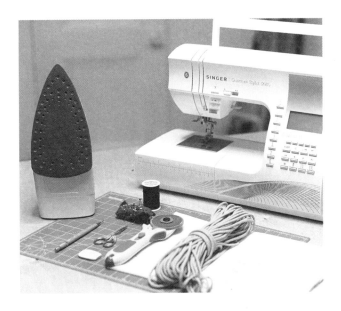

Step 1: Patterning

Each bag is made from a single, long, narrow rectangle of fabric, which is folded in half before it is sewn shut. Try the following sizes:

- Small Bags 40 × 25 cm (16 × 10 in) rectangle
- Medium Bags 60 × 38 cm (24 × 15 in) rectangle
- Large Bags 80 × 50 cm (32 × 20 in) rectangle

Once you make one bag, you'll find that the pattern is super easy to scale to your needs.

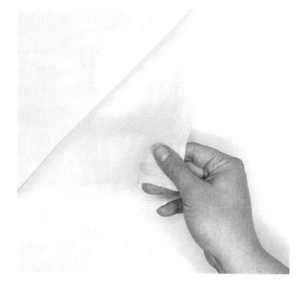

Step 2:
Cutting

Start by washing and drying your fabric, and then press with an iron on the setting appropriate for your textile. If you're unsure what your fabric is, then start with the iron at a low temperature and slowly turn up the heat until the fabric is pressing nicely.

Once the fabric is completely smooth, cut out a long rectangle to the required size and then fold this in half. Pin each of the long sides together.

On one of the long sides, measure 7.5 cm (3 in) down from the opening and mark with a pen or some tailor's chalk. This will later become the opening for the drawstring to slip through.

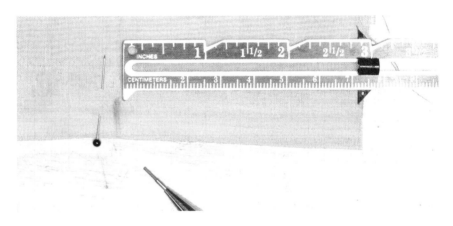

Step 3: Sewing

Begin by sewing the long side without the opening. When one side is sewn shut, rotate the bag and sew the remaining long seam, stopping short of the marking for the opening of the bag. I used an overlocking stitch to prevent any potential fabric fray, but zigzag stitch is also fine if your machine doesn't overlock.

To create the drawstring's cord chase, fold over each edge of the opening by about 5 mm (¼ in), then press and pin as shown in the picture. Once the drawstring edge is sewn down, complete a zigzag or overlock stitch around the top edge of the bag to prevent fraying.

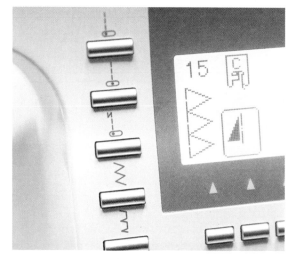

Tip:

Don't be afraid to personalise your bag! Why not try an embroidery tutorial on YouTube to give the bag an extra special feel?

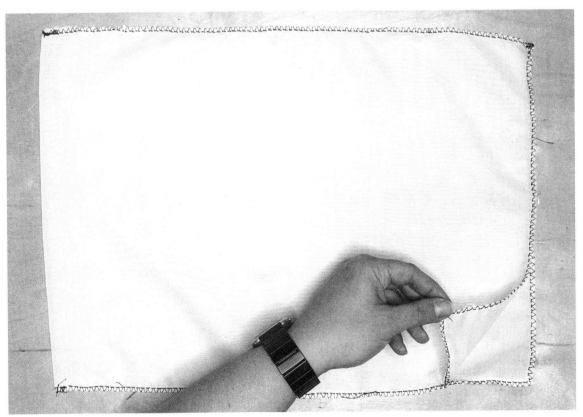

Step 4: Adding the drawstring

To create the cord chase for the drawstring, fold the top edge down by 4 cm (1½ in) and pin the edge back on the bag. I used a seam gauge to make fast work of pinning.

Once all the pins are in, press the top edge with an iron to make sewing down the flap easier. When you're ready to use the sewing machine, use a straight stitch to sew down the bound edge 4 cm (1½ in) away from the end of the bag. To sew a circular seam, you may need to take the free arm off your machine to work a tighter circumference.

When the seam is complete, measure out a length of cord that will fit through the chase, plus a little extra to cut down once the end is knotted. Connect a cord stopper through the end and pull through the cord chase.

Once the cord is coming out of both ends, thread both ends of the cord through the cord stopper and make a knotted end. I used paracord, which needs to be burned after it is cut to prevent it from fraying. It's always fun when a sewing project necessitates a little bit of fire.

Tip:

Make bags in different coloured fabric for different types of produce – try to source end-of-roll or upcycled fabric wherever possible.

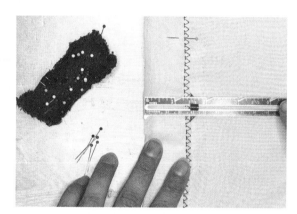

Keep it fresh!

That's it! Make a set in different sizes for all your bulk bag needs! It's a good idea to wash these bags from time to time. To clean the bags, soak them for 20 minutes in a solution of 3 parts water to 1 part vinegar. Then add 1 teaspoon of bicarbonate of soda and give the bags a gentle squeeze. Rinse under running water, then hang to dry.

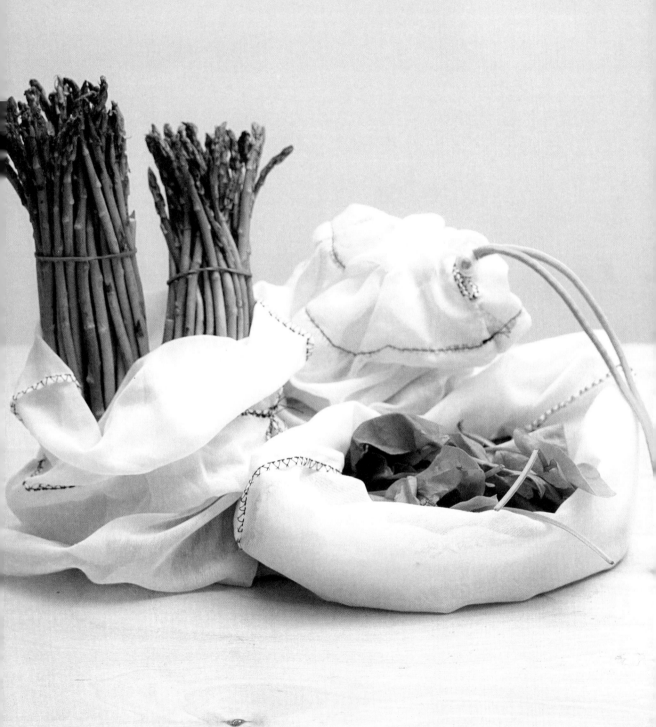

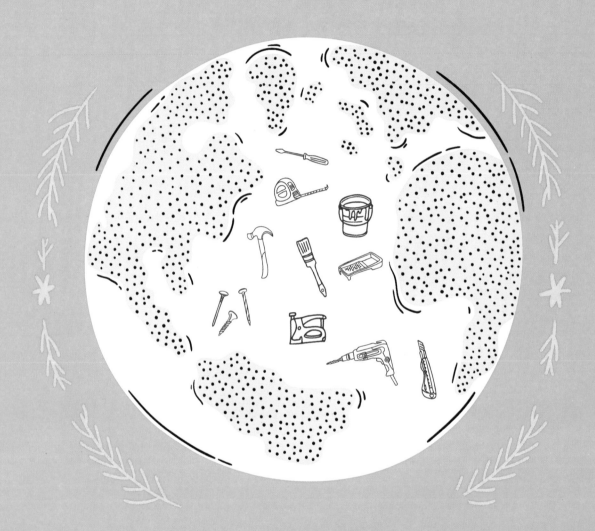

Tools of the sustainable maker

To complete the projects in this book you'll see a few tools come up over and over again. These are the tools that get used the most when upcycling old goods and for few other repair essentials you'll definitely be glad you have them around when you need to diagnose a fix.
- Cordless drill
- Circular saw (highly recommend a cordless one, but they aren't as powerful for thick pieces of timber)
- Precision screwdriver set (is used for eyeglasses, but with more interchangeable bits)
- Hot glue gun
- Pliers
- Sewing machine or a good hand-sewing kit
- Two-part fast-curing epoxy
- Paintbrushes
- Masking tape
- Soldering iron and multimeter – once you learn some basic electronics skills, it's easy to repair your own tech items and even home appliances

Workshop safety

It should also be noted that when it comes to using power tools, it is super important to use the personal protection recommended by the tool manufacturer. Investing in a good pair of safety glasses, durable work gloves, boots and a face shield has been crucial to my upcycling practice and recommended to any maker or hobbyist.

Have fun and keep learning!

Beyond the scope of these sustainable projects, I hope you're also inspired to go out into your community and learn about the ecological needs of your town. Learn how you can support some of the urban wildlife in your area, or participate in protecting the zones around your local water source.

Resources

Taking care of your items

Living more sustainably means becoming a steward of your items. If fabric rips, patch and sew it. If a bowl breaks, glue it back together, or use the broken pieces in your garden as mosaic or as drainage for pots. When wobbly furniture finally gives, create a new support for it or disassemble the broken item and salvage timber or even hardware like screws and bolts to use in future projects.

Now all of this may seem like a slippery slope into a hoarding situation and, quite frankly, it can be – consider carefully what you bring into your own ecosystem of stuff. Practicing sustainability is an exercise in challenging your consumption practices first, and your recycling and disposal practices second.

Smart purchasing

Start looking at labels to see if items are made with durable materials and consider the packaging each item you bring into your home comes in. Challenge yourself to see if you can go a day, a week, a month, without using something from a plastic container or made with petroleum products.

Buy used

Next time you're ready to buy a shiny new toy or garment – if you absolutely need the item, go look for it used first in a thrift shop or online on Etsy. Ebay and Craigslist can be a great way to save things like tech gear and furniture from the landfill too.

In writing this book, I asked many friends if they feel uncomfortable finding used goods, and most of them responded by saying they love thrifting, but that it's hard to find "good stuff" for your home or wardrobe. That is by design – a feature, not a bug – of consumption. Retailers would never make any money if folks weren't always buying the latest and greatest items from them, but there is a pivot happening where consumers are getting wiser about saving the planet and willing to do the extra footwork to find what they need from their local community to source gently used and refurbished stuff.

Thinking ahead

With any brand-new purchase that is made, it's important to understand the implications of where that material came from, how many emissions went into the air for the item to get to your door, and how you will eventually recycle or reuse this item when it is no longer of use to you. This mental reframing of sustainable choices applies to everything from food scraps going to compost, all the way to washing machines being repaired, or their metals and electronics being properly disposed of with using city's municipal waste service.

If you have clothes you'd like to donate, see if the organization you're donating to also offers garment and textile recycling, or works with a textile recycler to make commercial rags.

Once you're in the habit of considering all the holistic systems that your choices touch as an individual, you'll find yourself making greener and more sustainable choices or even becoming a climate activist.

Share your work!

It's hard work, but this is how we're going to collectively save our planet. Good thing you're perfect for the job! If you make any of the projects from this book or get inspired to make something sustainable on your own, share it! Please find us on the web and share your creation with @audreyobscura and @welbeckpublish.

Happy making!

Index

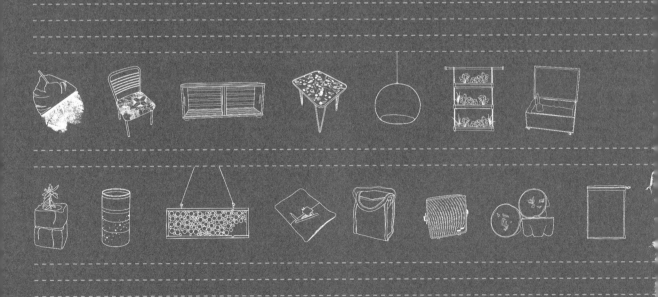